BEHAVIORAL BIOLOGY

AN INTERNATIONAL SERIES

Series editors

James L. McGaugh	**John C. Fentress**	**Joseph P. Hegman**
Department of Psychobiology	*Department of Psychology*	*Department of Zoology*
University of California	*Dalhousie University*	*The University of Iowa*
Irvine, California	*Halifax, Canada*	*Iowa City, Iowa*

Psychobiology
of Stress *A Study of Coping Men*

Psychobiology
of Stress A Study of Coping Men

Edited by
HOLGER URSIN
Institute of Psychology
University of Bergen
Bergen, Norway

EIVIND BAADE
Psychological Services of the Norwegian Armed Forces
Oslo, Norway

SEYMOUR LEVINE
Department of Psychiatry and Behavioral Sciences
Stanford University School of Medicine
Stanford, California

ACADEMIC PRESS
New York   San Francisco   London   1978
A Subsidiary of Harcourt Brace Jovanovich, Publishers

ACADEMIC PRESS, INC.
111 Fifth Avenue, New York, New York 10003

United Kingdom Edition published by
ACADEMIC PRESS, INC. (LONDON) LTD.
24/28 Oval Road, London NW1   7DX

Library of Congress Cataloging in Publication Data

Main entry under title:

Psychobiology of stress.

   (Behavioral biology series)
   Includes bibliographies.
   1. Stress (Physiology) 2. Parachuting--Physiologi-
cal aspects. 3. Psychobiology. 4. Norway. Haeren--
Parachute troops. I. Ursin, Holger. II. Baade,
Eivind. III. Levine, Seymour. IV. Series.
[DNLM: 1. Stress, Psychological--Physiology.
2. Psychophysiology. 3. Parachuting. 4. Aviation
medicine. 5. Military medicine. 6. Psychology,
Military. 7. Hormones--Physiology. WD730 P974]
QP82.2.S8P79   612'.042   78-8119
ISBN 0-12-709250-1

PRINTED IN THE UNITED STATES OF AMERICA